Science Sight Word Readers™

Rain Forests

by Megan Duhamel

ISBN 978-0-545-24805-1

Photographs © 2010: cover: Corbis Images/Chris Cheadle; back cover top: iStockphoto/Mark Kostich; back cover bottom: iStockphoto/Simone van den Berg; page 1: iStockphoto/Brandon Alms; page 2 main: ShutterStock, Inc./Ralph Loesche; page 2 inset: iStockphoto/ideeone; page 3: iStockphoto/Roberto Zocchi; page 4: ShutterStock, Inc./worldswildlifewonders; page 5: Corbis Images/Frans Lanting; page 6: iStockphoto/Jacques Croizer; page 7: Getty Images/Chris Stein; page 8: Photo Researchers, NY/Bill Love; page 9: Minden Pictures/Pete Oxford; page 10: ShutterStock, Inc./Cathy Keifer; page 11: iStockphoto/Morley Read; page 12: iStockphoto/Simone van den Berg; page 13: ShutterStock, Inc./Luis Louro; page 14: Corbis Images/Chris Cheadle; page 15: ShutterStock, Inc./Ralph Loesche; page 16: Photo Researchers, NY/Jany Sauvanet.

Photo research by Ed Kasche; Design by Holly Grundon

12 11 10 9 8 7 6 5 4 3 2 10 11 12 13 14 15/0

Printed in the U.S.A. 40

First printing, November 2010

SCHOLASTIC INC.

NEW YORK • TORONTO • LONDON • AUCKLAND
SYDNEY • MEXICO CITY • NEW DELHI • HONG KONG

Welcome to the **rain** forest!

You **will find** animals of every color in the **rain** forest.

You **will find** this red animal in the **rain** forest.

You **will find** this **other** red animal, too.

You **will find** this blue animal in the **rain** forest.

You **will find** this **other** blue animal, too.

You **will find** this yellow animal in the **rain** forest.

You **will find** this **other** yellow animal, too.

You **will find** this green animal in the **rain** forest.

You **will find** this **other** green animal, too.

You **will find** this orange animal in the **rain** forest.

You **will find** animals of every color in the **rain** forest!

Sight Word Review

Point to each sight word. Then read it aloud.

Sight Word Fill-ins

Use one sight word from the box to finish each sentence.

find	**other**
rain	**will**

1. The ________ forest is full of colorful creatures.
2. You ________ see lots of tall trees in the rain forest.
3. Some creatures are green and ________ ones are red.
4. Can you ________ more facts about the rain forest?

ANSWERS: 1. rain 2. will 3. other 4. find

All About Rain Forests

Ask a grown-up to read this with you.

sloth

It is warm and humid in a rain forest because it rains almost every day. This causes plants to grow thickly and trees to grow tall, forming homes for all kinds of creatures.

Different animals live in different parts of the rain forest. Toucans and howler monkeys make their homes in the treetops. This is called the rain forest canopy. Jaguars and sloths live lower down in the trees. This part of the rain forest is called the understory. Plenty of animals also live on the rain forest floor: insects and snakes and large mammals, such as tapirs.

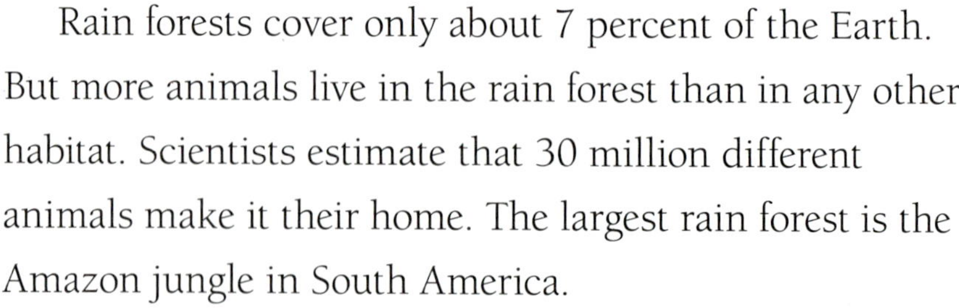

Rain forests cover only about 7 percent of the Earth. But more animals live in the rain forest than in any other habitat. Scientists estimate that 30 million different animals make it their home. The largest rain forest is the Amazon jungle in South America.

Many of the world's rain forests are in danger. People are cutting down the trees. If rain forests disappear, the amazing animals that call them home will also disappear.